A GEOGRAPHY OF BRITISH GUIANA.

BY THE
REV. JOHN FOREMAN,
BERBICE.

LONDON:
JOHN SNOW, 35, PATERNOSTER ROW.
1863.

PREFACE.

During the seventeen years that I have been connected with the education of the young in Berbice, I have often felt the want of a school-book which should give to the children some information concerning *their own country.*

That want I have endeavoured in the following pages to supply, and they contain a much *larger amount of information about British Guiana* than any other school-book in use in this colony.

The book has been drawn up in its present form, from the conviction, that by the great majority of the scholars in this country, the facts will be thus more easily retained.

I would recommend teachers to use this book also for dictation and spelling exercises. The writing out by their scholars of the names of six or more places and things mentioned therein, and then committing them to memory, will be found a valuable lesson. The correct spelling of the names of places in their own country by the scholars, is an object worthy the attention of every teacher.

JOHN FOREMAN.

BERBICE, 1863.

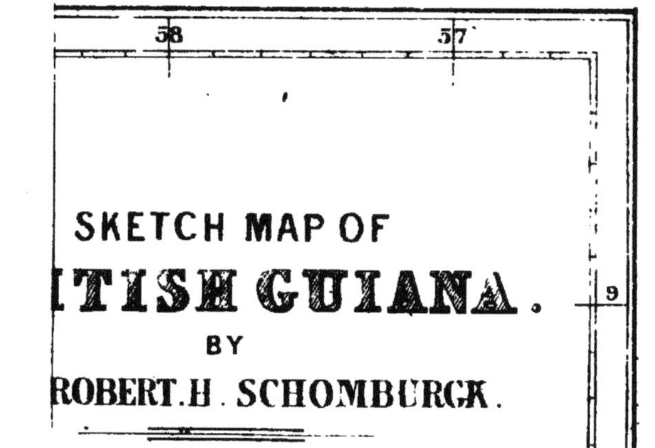
58
57
9
SKETCH MAP OF
ITISH GUIANA.
BY
ROBERT.H. SCHOMBURGK.
or Great Cat.

A

GEOGRAPHY OF BRITISH GUIANA.

Q. What is Geography?

A. A description of the Earth.

Q. Who formed the Earth?

A. "God created the Heavens and the Earth."

Q. How did God do this?

A. "By the word of his power." "He spake, and it was done."

Q. What *shape* is the Earth?

A. Round.

Q. What is the *outside* of the Earth called?

A. Its surface.

Q. What does the *surface* of the Earth consist of?

A. Land and water.

Q. How much of the Earth's surface is covered with water?

A. About three quarters.

Q. What is the largest division of land called?

A. A Continent.

Name the Continents.

Europe, Asia, Africa, North America, South America, and Australia.

Point them out on the Map of the World.

Q. On which of these Continents do you live?

A. South America.

Q. What *name* is given to this part of South America?

A. British Guiana.

Q. Can you point it out on the Map?

Q. What is the *Latitude* and *Longitude* of British Guiana?

A. It is situated between 1 degree and 8 degrees of North Latitude, and between 57 and 61 degrees of West Longitude.

Q. What is *Latitude?*

A. Distance from the *Equator*, North or South.

Q. What is the *Equator?*

A. An imaginary line, round the centre of the Earth.

Q. What is *Longitude?*

A. Distance East or West from a given place.

Q. Why was it called *Guiana?*

A. From a tribe of Indians called "Guayanoes."

Q. Why is it called *British* Guiana?

A. Because it belongs to Great Britain.

Q. Can you give any other reason?

A. To distinguish it from *Dutch* Guiana and *French* Guiana.

Point out *Dutch* Guiana and *French* Guiana on the map.

Q. What else is Dutch Guiana called?

A. Surinam.

Q. To what country does it belong?

A. Holland.

Q. Where is Holland?

A. In Europe.

Point it out on the map.

Q. What other name is French Guiana known by?

A. Cayenne.

Q. To what country does it belong?

A. France.

Q. Where is France?

A. In Europe.

Point it out on the map.

Show with your hand *in which direction* Dutch Guiana and French Guiana lie, from this school.

Q. Is Dutch Guiana or French Guiana *nearest* to British Guiana?

A. Dutch Guiana.

Q. What *separates* British Guiana from Dutch Guiana?

A. The river Corentyne.

Point it out on the map.

Q. What is the largest division of water called?

A. An Ocean.

Q. How many oceans are there?

A. Five.

Name them.

The Pacific, Atlantic, Indian, Arctic, and Antarctic Oceans.

Point them out on the map.

Q. *Which Ocean* washes the shores of British Guiana?

A. The Atlantic Ocean.

Point towards it.

Q. What country lies to the *West* of British Guiana?

A. Venezuela.

Q. What is the name of the country to the *South* of British Guiana?

A. Brazil.

Find Brazil and Venezuela on the map.

Point in the *direction* of Brazil.

Point in the *direction* of Venezuela.

Q. Tell me how British Guiana is bounded on the *North*.

A. By the Atlantic Ocean.

Q. On the *South?*

A. By Brazil.

Q. On the *East?*

A. By Surinam.

Q. On the *West?*

A. By Venezuela.

Q. What is the *length* of British Guiana from East to West?

A. Two hundred and eighty miles.

Q. What is the *breadth* of British Guiana from North to South?

A. It varies from 300 to 450 miles.

Q. How many rods are there in a mile?

A. About 142.

Q. How many *square miles* does British Guiana contain?

A. At least 84,000.

Q. What is meant by a *square* mile?

A. A piece of land that is a mile in length, and a mile in breadth.

Q. What is a *River?*

A. A stream of fresh water.

Give me the names of the *principal rivers* of British Guiana.

Essequibo, Demerara, Berbice, and Corentyne.

Point them out on the map.

Q. Where does the river Essequibo *commence?*

A. In the Acarai mountains.

Q. What is its *length?*

A. About 600 miles.

Q. How *far* up the Essequibo can ships go?

A. Fifty miles.

Q. What prevents their going farther?

A. A ridge of rocks stretching across the river.

Q. What do these rocks cause?

A. The Falls.

Q. How *wide* is the Essequibo where it flows into the ocean?

A. About 20 miles.

Q. What are situated at the *mouth* of the Essequibo?

A. A number of islands.

Q. What *size* are these islands?

A. Some of them are from 12 to 15 miles long.

Q. What is an Island?

A. Land surrounded by water.

Name the principal islands in the Essequibo.

Wakenaam, Leguan, Hog Island, Tiger Island, and Troolie Island.

Q. Do people *live* upon these islands?

A. Yes, and there are sugar estates upon them.

Turn your face *towards* the river Essequibo.

Point out the river Essequibo on the map.

Q. Where does the river Demerara begin?

A. This is known only by the Indians.

Q. To what distance can ships ascend the Demerara?

A. Seventy-five miles.

Q. What prevents their going farther?

A. The falls.

Q. How *wide* is the river Demerara at its mouth?

A. Two miles.

Turn your face towards the river Demerara.

Point it out on the map.

Q. Where does the river *Berbice* begin?

A. This has not yet been ascertained.

Q. How far can good-sized vessels ascend it?

A. One hundred miles.

Q. How far can a schooner go?

A. One hundred and seventy-five miles.

Q. What would stop the schooner at that distance?

A. The falls.

Q. What remarkable *flower* was discovered in the upper part of the river Berbice?

A. The Victoria Regia lily.

Q. What is the size of the *flower* and of the *leaves* of the Victoria Regia?

A. The flower is larger than a man's head, and the leaves are five feet across.

Q. How *wide* is the river Berbice at its mouth?

A. Upwards of two miles.

Q. What *island* is situated at the entrance of the river Berbice?

A. Crab Island.

Q. Is it inhabited?

A. No.

Turn your face towards the river Berbice.

Point it out on the map.

Q. Where does the river *Corentyne* commence?

A. About 25 miles from the source of the Essequibo.

Q. What is the *source* of a river?

A. The place where it begins.

Q. What is the *length* of the river Corentyne?

A. Probably 600 miles.

Q. To what distance can small vessels ascend it?

A. One hundred and fifty miles.

Q. How wide is it at its *junction* with the Ocean?

A. At least 10 miles.

Q. Has it any islands?

A. A great many.

Turn your face in the *direction* of the Corentyne.

Point it out on the map.

Q. What are the *smaller* rivers of British Guiana called?

A. Creeks.

Give the *names* of some of them.

Pomeroon, Bocrasiri, Mahaica, Mahaicony, Abary, and Canje.

Q. How many of these *flow* into the Atlantic Ocean?

A. All except the Canje, which flows into the river Berbice.

Q. Are there any still smaller streams running into these rivers and creeks?

A. Yes, an immense number.

Q. What is a *Mountain?*

A. Land and rock rising to a great height.

Q. Are there any mountains in this colony?

A. Yes, far in the interior.

Name the highest one.

Roraima.

Q. What does the Indian name Roraima mean?

A. Red rock.

Q. How *high* above the level of the sea is it?

A. Seven thousand five hundred feet.

Q. How high is the church steeple, or the top of the estates chimney?

Q. How *many times higher*, *then*, is the peak of Roraima?

Q. In which part of the colony do the mountains approach nearest to the sea?

A. In Essequibo.

Q. What other elevations are there?

A. The sand-hills.

Q. Where are they situated?

A. About forty miles from the sea, and still further inland.

Q. What *height* are they?

A. From 30 to 120 feet.

Q. What is the character of the country from the sand-hills to the ocean?

A. Flat.

Q. What is the nature of the *climate?*

A. Hot, but cooled by the trade wind, and not liable to great changes of temperature.

Q. How many *seasons* are there in this country?

A. Two.

Q. What are they?

A. The wet season and the dry season.

Q. When are the *wet* seasons?

A. From December to February, and from April to August.

Q. When are the *dry* seasons?

A. From August to December, and from February to April.

Q. In which *months* does the *most* rain fall?

A. May and June.

Q. Which month is generally the *driest?*

A. October.

Q. What part of the colony is under cultivation?

A. Only a narrow strip along the coast, and some places on the banks of the principal rivers.

Q. What is the nature of the soil?

A. Very fertile.

Q. How can you prove that?

A. Because manure is scarcely ever used, and yet the land yields abundantly.

Q. What is the *principal plant* cultivated?

A. The sugar cane.

Q. What is obtained from it?

A. Sugar, molasses, and rum.

Q. How is *Sugar made?*

A. The canes, being cut down, are conveyed to the buildings in punts. The juice is squeezed out of the canes by powerful rollers. It is then clarified, and boiled in large coppers, to a certain thickness, and then placed in coolers.

Q. Is all the sugar in the colony thus manufactured?

A. No, Vacuum-pans, Gadsden-pans, and other improved methods, are used on many estates.

Q. What is the sugar-cane called, *after* the juice has been squeezed out of it?

A. Megass.

Q. Of what use is it?

A. After being dried in the megass logie, it is used for fuel.

Q. What is *Molasses?*

A. The thick juice that drains from the sugar.

Q. What quantity of molasses drains from a hogshead of sugar?

A. About 60 gallons.

Q. What is done with the molasses?

A. In England, it is used in the manufacture of white sugar, beer, and for other purposes. In North America, it is clarified and eaten with corn meal, dressed in a variety of ways.

Q. What is *Rum?*

A. A strong intoxicating liquor.

Q. How is it obtained?

A. By distilling molasses, the skimmings of the cane juice, etc.

Q. What *quantity* of sugar is made in this colony every year?

A. About 65,000 hogsheads.

Q. What *quantity* of sugar does each *hogshead* contain?

A. About a ton.

Q. How much is a ton?

A. Twenty hundred weight, or 2240 lbs.

Repeat Avoirdupois weight.

Q. What is done with all this sugar?

A. It is nearly all exported.

Q. What do you mean by *exported?*

A. Sent out of the country.

Q. What *quantity* of Molasses is exported annually?

A. About 4000 casks.

Q. How much does each molasses cask *hold?*

A. About 90 gallons.

Q. How many *quarts* are there in a gallon?

A. Four.

Tell me something that will *hold a quart.*

Q. What *quantity* of *Rum* is exported every year from British Guiana?

A. About 26,000 puncheons.

Q. How many *gallons* does a *puncheon* of Rum contain?

A. About 100 gallons.

Q. What quantity of Rum is *drunk* in the colony annually?

A. About 120,000 gallons.

Name some other articles that are *exported* from this colony.

Timber, Shingles, Firewood, Charcoal, Cocoa Nuts, Fish glue, and Skins.

Q. From what *fish* is the "*fish glue*" obtained?

A. The Gilbacker.

Q. What other products were formerly exported in large quantities?

A. Cotton and coffee.

Q. What *Plants* are grown as articles of food?

A. The Plantain, Yams of various kinds, sweet and bitter Cassava, sweet Potatoes, Tannias, Ochroes, Corn, Pumpkins, Rice, and Peas, of many different sorts.

Q. How is the *Plantain* used?

A. In its green state, mostly. Sometimes when yellow, and also when sliced and dried.

Q. What are the *plantains* when boiled and pounded called?

A. Foofoo.

Q. What are the *sliced* and dried plantains called?

A. After being pounded, it is called Conquin-tay, and plantain meal.

Q. What are the principal *Fruit-trees* grown?

A. The Cocoa-nut, Banana, Orange, Lime, Mango, Sour-sop, Star-apple, Sugar-apple, Mamme, Tamarind, Alligator-pear, Sappodilla, and Guava.

Q. What is made from the Cocoa-nut?

A. Cocoa-nut oil, which is largely used by the Coolies.

Q. What *other oils* are made in the colony?

A. Crab-oil and Castor-oil.

Q. What is *Crab-oil* made from?

A. The seeds of the Crab-wood tree.

Q. What is it used for?

A. For burning; as a hair-oil, and for the skin diseases of horses and cattle.

Q. What is *Castor-oil* made from?

A. The seeds of the Castor-oil plant.

Q. For what purpose is it used?

A. As a medicine.

Q. How are these various oils made?

A. By grating or pounding the seeds, then boiling them in water, and skimming off the oil as it rises to the surface.

Q. From what plants is *Starch* manufactured in this colony?

A. Arrow-root, Sweet Cassava, Bitter Cassava, and Tous-les-mois or Buckshot.

Q. How is the *Starch* procured?

A. The roots are dug, washed, grated, strained through a cloth into a cask, at the bottom of which the starch is allowed to settle. It is then taken out and dried in the sun.

Q. What is the *Arrow-root* starch made in this colony used for?

A. As pap, but principally for stiffening clothes.

Q. From what other plants *might* starch be obtained?

A. From the different kinds of Yams, Sweet Potatoes, and Tannias.

Q. For what purpose is the *Bitter* Cassava generally grown?

A. To make Cassava Bread.

Q. How is Cassava *bread* made?

A. By grating the root, squeezing out the juice, baking, and drying in the sun.

Q. Is anything done with the *juice*?

A. It is boiled, and is then called Cassareep.

Q. What is *Cassareep* used for?

A. In making pepper-pot, and also for making sauces, and gravies.

Q. What portion of the colony is inhabited?

A. Only the end nearest the sea.

Q. What does the rest of the colony consist of?

A. Immense Savannahs, and extensive forests of valuable trees.

Q. To what purpose might these Savannahs be applied?

A. The rearing of thousands of cattle, sheep, and horses.

Q. What are the *principal Woods* used either in the colony or exported?

A. Greenheart, Mora, Bullet-tree, Wallaba, and Crab-wood.

Q. From what part of the colony is *Greenheart* principally obtained?

A. Essequibo.

Q. To what purposes is it applied?

A. House-frames, stellings, and the planking of vessels.

Q. What is prepared from the *bark* and *seeds* of the Greenheart tree?

A. A valuable medicine in fevers, called Bibirine.

Q. What use do the Indians make of the *seeds* of the Greenheart tree?

A. When food is scarce, they grate the seeds, and mixing the starch thus obtained with decayed Wallaba wood, eat it.

Q. To what height does the Mora tree grow?

A. From 120 to 150 feet.

Q. Which is *highest*, the *Mora* tree or the estates chimney?

Describe the *wood* of the Mora tree.

It is tough, close, difficult to split, and not liable to dry rot.

Q. For what purposes is it especially suitable?

A. For the keels, timbers, beams, and knees of ships.

Q. What is the *bark* of the Mora tree used for?

A. Tanning.

Q. What is *tanning?*

A. The process by which skins are made into leather.

Q. What are the *seeds* of the Mora tree used for?

A. For food by the Indians in times of scarcity, and also as a medicine in cases of dysentery.

Q. In what part of the colony is the *Bullet-tree* most abundant?

A. In Berbice.

Q. For what purposes is it used?

A. The frames of houses, wheel-spokes, palings, etc.

Q. What does the *milk* of the Bullet-tree contain?

A. A substance resembling India-rubber, and called Balata.

Q. In what part of the colony are *Wallaba* trees found?

A. They are abundant throughout the colony.

Describe the *wood* of the Wallaba tree.

It is hard, heavy, splits freely and smoothly, and is of a deep red colour.

Q. What is it principally used for?

A. The making of shingles.

Q. What are *Shingles?*

A. Thin pieces of wood, 3 or 4 inches broad, and 21 inches long.

Q. What are they used for?

A. For covering the roofs and sides of houses, and other buildings.

Q. What else does the Wallaba tree yield?

A. An oil, of great value in cuts and bruises.

Q. Where are *Crab-wood* trees to be found?

A. In all parts of the colony.

Q. What is *Crab-wood* used for?

A. Masts, and spars of vessels; floors, partitions, and doors of houses, and articles of furniture.

Q. Is the *bark* of any use?

A. It is used for tanning.

Q. What is obtained from the *seeds* of the Crab-wood tree?

A. Crab-oil.

Q. Do our forests contain many other trees, besides those you have mentioned?

A. A very great number, suited for useful, ornamental, and medicinal purposes.

Q. What are *Minerals?*

A. Things dug out of the Earth, such as Gold, Silver, Iron, and Tin.

Q. Are there any *minerals* in British Guiana?

A. The mountainous portion of the colony is so far from the inhabited parts, that it cannot be positively asserted.

Q. What minerals is it *supposed* may be obtained there?

A. Gold and Iron.

Q. Why *Gold?*

A. Because the gold-fields of Venezuela are close upon the borders of this colony.

Q. Why *Iron?*

A. Because the water of the wells is strongly impregnated with iron.

Name the principal *wild* animals of this colony *injurious to man.*

The Jaguar or Tiger, Puma, Tiger-cat, Alligator, Salempenter, Crab-dog, Yawarry, and Snakes.

Name some of the *wild* animals *useful* to man.

Water-haas, Peccary, Deer, Labba, and Iguana.

Q. What *wild birds* are *injurious* to man?

A. The different species of Hawks.

Q. What *wild birds* are used for food by man?

A. Wild Ducks, Pigeons, Parrots, Herons, Cranes, Currie Curries, Gauldings, and Spoonbills.

Q. What do the rivers and the sea furnish man with?

A. Large quantities of fish of many different kinds, Turtles, and also the Sea-cow.

Q. What are the principal *insects* of British Guiana?

A. Ants, Beetles, Bête-rouge, Butterflies, Centipedes, Chigoes, Cockroaches, Marabunters, Mosquitoes, Sandflies, Scorpions, Spiders, and Tarantulas.

Q. From what countries do we *import* goods?

A. From Great Britain, the United States, India, New Brunswick, etc.

Point out these countries on the map.

Q. What is the *meaning* of import?

A. To bring in.

Q. What do we *import* from *Great Britain?*

A. Books, Clothing, Furniture, Medicines, Tools, Crockery-ware, etc.

Q. What do we obtain from the *United States?*

A. Flour, Corn, Corn Meal, Biscuits, Salt Beef, Salt Pork, Horses, Mules, and Ice.

Q. What do we obtain from *India?*

A. Rice, Gram, Ghee, and Ganje.

Q. What do we get from *New Brunswick?*

A. Lumber and Salt Fish.

POLITICAL FACTS.

Q. Who were the *first* Europeans that settled in this Colony?

A. The Dutch.

Q. In *what year* did this take place?

A. In 1580.

Q. How long is that since?

Q. When was this colony first taken possession of by the English?

A. In 1781.

Q. How many years is that ago?

Q. When was this Colony restored to Holland?

A. In 1783.

Q. When was it last taken by the English?

A. In 1803.

Q. What *number of years* has elapsed since then?

Q. How was the cultivation carried on at that time?

A. By slaves.

Q. Where were they obtained from?

A. Africa.

Q. When was the *slave trade* abolished?

A. In 1814.

Q. In what year did the "*Apprenticeship*" begin?

A. In 1834.

Q. How long is that since?

Q. How many slaves were there in this colony at that time?

eenwich.

A. 82,824.

Q. When did "*Freedom*" take place?

A. On the 1st of August, 1838.

Q. How many years ago is that?

Q. Are there slaves in any of the British Colonies now?

A. None.

Q. When were the Colonies of Demerara, Essequibo, and Berbice united?

A. In 1831.

Q. What *name* was then given to the Colony?

A. That of British Guiana.

Q. How is British Guiana divided?

A. Into counties and parishes.

Q. How *many Counties* are there?

A. Three.

Name them.

Demerara, Essequibo, and Berbice.

Show them on the map.

Q. In *which* County do you reside? Point with your hand in the direction of the other two Counties.

Q. Where does the County of Essequibo begin and end?

A. It begins at the river Barima, and ends at the Boerasiri Creek.

Q. What *distance* is it from one end to the other of the County of Essequibo?

A. About 120 miles.

Q. Where does the *County of Demerara* begin and end?

A. It commences at Boerasiri Creek, and ends at the Abary Creek.

Q. What *distance* apart are these two creeks?

A. About sixty-five miles.

Q. How far does the *County of Berbice* extend?

A. From the Abary Creek to the River Corentyne.

Q. What is the *distance* between these two rivers?

A. About ninety-five miles.

Q. What is the population of Essequibo?

A. 27,959.

Q. What number of persons live in Demerara?

A. 91,369.

Q. How many of these reside in George Town?

A. 29,174.

Q. How many inhabitants has Berbice?

A. 28,698.

Q. How many of these live in New Amsterdam?

A. 4579.

Q. Do these numbers include the *Indians?*

A. No.

Q. How many Indians are there in the Colony?

A. It is supposed about 7000.

Q. What is the total of the population by the Census of 1861?

A. 155,907.

Q. Who *compose* the population of British Guiana?

A. Creoles, or persons born in the Colony, Africans, Chinese, Coolies from Calcutta and Madras, Portuguese, and other Europeans and Indians.

Q. Is there *room* in this Colony for many more people besides those already living here?

A. Yes, for hundreds of thousands.

Q. Into how many *parishes* is British Guiana divided?

A. Seventeen.

Name the parishes in Essequibo.

The Trinity, Saint John's, Saint James's, Saint Peter's, and part of Saint Luke's.

Q. What parishes are situated in Demerara?

A. Part of Saint Luke's, Saint Swithin's, Saint Mark's, Saint Matthew's, Saint George's, also called Saint Andrew's, Saint Paul's, and Saint Mary's.

Q. What are the names of the parishes in Berbice?

A. Saint Michael's, Saint Catherine's, Saint Clement's, All Saints, Saint Patrick's, and Saint Saviour's.

Q. *Which* parish do you live in? What is the name of the next parish to the right hand of the school? What is the name of the parish on the left hand?

Q. What is the name of our most Gracious Sovereign?

A. Her Majesty Queen Victoria.

Q. Who is appointed to act for the Queen in this Colony?

A. His Excellency the Governor.

Q. What is our present Governor's name?

A. Francis Hincks, Esq., C.B.

Q. By whom are our laws made?

A. By the Court of Policy.

Q. How is the *Court of Policy* composed?

A. Of five of the principal officers of the Government, and five other gentlemen.

Name the *Official Members* of the Court of Policy.

The Governor, the Chief Justice, the Attorney General, the Government Secretary, and the Administrator General.

Q. How are the *other five* gentlemen appointed?

A. Whenever a vacancy occurs, the College of Electors send up to the Court of Policy the names of two persons, one of whom is selected by that Court as the new member.

Q. For what *period* are the members of the Court of Policy chosen?

A. For no specific period, but the *senior* Elective member retires at the close of the Annual Session of the Combined Court.

Q. What *qualification* must members of the Court of Policy possess?

A. They must be owners of land in a state of cultivation, Protestants, and able to speak Dutch. This last has long since ceased to be one of the qualifications.

Q. Of *whom* does the College of Electors consist?

A. Of seven gentlemen elected for life.

Q. How are they chosen?

A. By public vote, the Colony being divided into electoral districts for the purpose.

Name the *districts* and the *number* of *members* allotted to each.

(1) County of Demerara, one member; (2) City of George Town, two members; (3) County of Essequibo, two members; (4) County of Berbice, one member; (5) Town of New Amsterdam, one member.

Q. What *qualification* is necessary to sit in the College of Electors?

A. The possession of 80 *acres of land*, 40 of which must be under cultivation, or *property*, the rent of which is $1200 per annum, or *income* of $1440 from trade or property in the Colony.

Q. Who *vote* at elections for members of the College of Electors?

A. Those who have three *acres of land* in cultivation, or *income* of $600 per annum, or *property* in George Town or New Amsterdam of the appraised value of $500, and are duly registered.

Q. How is the *Income* and *Expenditure* of the Colony settled?

A. By the Combined Court.

Q. How is the *Combined* Court formed?

A. Of all the members of the Court of Policy and six other gentlemen.

Q. What are these six gentlemen *called?*

A. Financial Representatives.

Q. What *power* does the Combined Court possess over the finances of the Colony?

A. That of *decreasing* or striking off any item on the Estimate, as prepared by the Court of Policy, and preparing the "Ways and Means."

Q. What is the *Estimate?*

A. An account of the money that will be required for various purposes for the year.

Q. What is meant by "*Ways and Means*"?

A. The various taxes by which the money that is required is to be raised.

Q. How are the Financial Representatives *chosen?*

A. One by each electoral district, except Essequibo (3), which chooses two.

Q. What qualification must a Financial Representative possess?

A. The same as a member of the College of Electors (see page 29).

Q. For what period are they chosen?

A. Two years.

Q. Who have the privilege of *voting* for Financial Representatives?

A. Those who are qualified to vote for members of the College of Electors (see page 29).

Q. How are the *affairs* of the city of George Town managed?

A. By the Mayor and Town Council.

Q. By whom is the Mayor appointed?

A. The members of the Town Council choose one of their own number as Mayor.

Q. For how *long* does the Mayor hold office?

A. For one year, but he can be reappointed.

Q. Of how many members does the Town Council consist?

A. Eleven, including the Mayor.

Q. How are they *elected?*

A. The city is divided, for this and other purposes, into districts called Wards.

Q. How many *Wards* are there?

A. Eleven.

Name the *first six Wards.*

(1) Kingston; (2) North Cuminsburg, West; (3) North Cuminsburg and Albert Town, East; (4) South Cuminsburg, West; (5) South Cuminsburg and Albert Town East; (6) Robb's Town.

Name the other *five* Wards.

(7) Columbia and Lacy Town; (8) New Town; (9) Stabroek; (10) Werkenrust; (11) Charlestown.

Q. How *many members* does each Ward choose?

A. One.

Q. For how many *years* are they elected?

A. Two years.

Q. What *qualification* must a member of the Town Council possess?

A. Premises within the city of George Town valued at $1500 and upwards.

Q. Who have the privilege of *voting* at the Election of Members of the Town Council?

A. Those who have premises in the city of Georgetown, of the appraised value of 250 dollars and upwards, and have been duly registered.

Q. How are the *affairs* of the town of New Amsterdam managed?

A. By the Board of Superintendence.

Q. Who form this Board?

A. Seven gentlemen, one of whom is chosen President by the others.

Q. What *qualification* is necessary?

A. The owning or representing of property in New Amsterdam worth at least 1000 dollars.

Q. For what *period* are they elected?

A. For about three years, as the two senior members retire every year, but may be re-elected.

Q. By *whom* are these gentlemen elected?

A. By those persons in New Amsterdam, whose property is valued at 400 dollars and upwards, and whose town taxes are duly paid.

Name the various *Courts of Justice* in the colony.

Magistrates' Courts, Inferior Civil Courts, Inferior Criminal Courts, Superior Civil Courts, and Superior Criminal Courts.

Q. Where are the *Magistrates'* Courts held?

A. At several places in each magisterial district.

Q. Where are the *Inferior Civil Courts* held?

A. In Georgetown, and New Amsterdam.

Q. Who *presides* in the Inferior Civil Court?

A. One of the Judges.

Q. Where are the Inferior *Criminal* Courts held?

A. In all three of the counties.

Q. Where are they held in Demerara?

A. At the public buildings in Georgetown, and at the Hague and Vreed-en-Hoop police stations.

Q. Where in *Essequibo?*

A. At Capoey police station.

Q. Where in *Berbice?*

A. At the Court-house, New Amsterdam, and at Fort Wellington and Albion police stations.

Q. How *often* are these courts held?

A. In Georgetown on the last Thursday in each month, and four times a year at all the other places.

Q. Who *presides* in the Inferior *Criminal* Courts?

A. One of the Judges, assisted by at least three Justices of the Peace.

Q. Who are *Justices of the Peace?*

A. A number of gentlemen throughout the colony, appointed to this office by His Excellency the Governor.

Q. Where are the *Supreme Civil* Courts held?

A. In Georgetown and New Amsterdam.

Q. How *often* does this Court sit?

A. Three times a year in Georgetown, and twice a year in New Amsterdam.

Q. By whom are the cases in the *Supreme Civil* Court *heard?*

A. By all three of the Judges, or by one Judge and a jury, or by a Judge alone.

Q. What causes all this difference?

A. The nature of the cases that have to come before the Court.

Q. Where are the Supreme *Criminal* Courts held?

A. In Georgetown, New Amsterdam, and in Essequibo.

Q. How *often* are they held?

A. Four times a year in Demerara, and twice a year in Essequibo and Berbice.

Q. By *whom* are the trials in the Supreme Criminal Courts heard?

A. By a judge and a jury of twelve men.

Q. Who compose the jury?

A. They are selected from a list of persons between the ages of twenty-one and sixty, who have an income of 96 dollars per annum from immoveable property, or of 192 dollars from leasehold property, or who occupy a house of the same value, or receive a salary of 720 dollars a year.

Q. Where are persons sentenced by the Supreme Criminal Court generally sent to?

A. The Penal settlement.

Q. Where is it situated?

A. At the junction of the river Mazzaruni with the Essequibo.

Q. What is it sometimes called on this account?

A. Mazzaruni.

Turn your *back* to it.

Q. What *denominations* of Christians are there in this colony?

A. The English Church, Scotch Church, Roman Catholics, Wesleyans, London Missionaries, Independents, and Brethren.

Q. How many of these are supported by *grants* from the colony?

A. The Ministers of the English and Scotch churches receive all their salaries from the colony. The Roman Catholic and Wesleyan churches have large sums voted to them, the appropriation of which is left to themselves.

Q. How are the ministers of the London Missionary Society, Independents, and Brethren supported?

A. By voluntary contributions.

Q. Have the above denominations any *Day Schools* connected with them?

A. Yes, all.

Q. Are these *Day Schools* all supported by Government grants?

A. No, the Ministers of the London Missionary Society, Independents (with one exception), and Brethren, do not receive Government aid.

Q. How then are their Day Schools supported?

A. By the school fees and voluntary contributions.

Printed for John Snow, London.

www.ingramcontent.com/pod-product-compliance
Lightning Source LLC
LaVergne TN
LVHW012019160826
845678LV00002B/917